توم وصوفيا يبدآن المدرسة
Tom and Sofia start School

Henriette Barkow

Priscilla Lamont
Arabic translation by Ayser Aljawad

توم   جاءتْ معلّمتي الجديدةُ إلى البيتِ. اِسمُها الآنسةُ روس. أخذتْ لنا صورةً فوتوغرافيةً لي ولوالدتي. ثم رسمتُ لها صورةً. قالتِ الآنسةُ روس إن صورتي ستعلق على حائطِ الصفِّ عندما تبدأ المدرسةُ.

Tom   My new teacher came to my home. Her name is Miss Ross. She took a photo of me and my mum. Then I did a drawing for her. Miss Ross said that my picture will be on the classroom wall when I start school.

قبلَ أُسْبوعٍ

صوفيا　　أَخَذَتْنا والدتي أنا وأُختي آنّا لِنتبضّعَ. قالتْ أن علَيْنا أنْ نشتريَ ثيابا
خاصةً للمدرسةِ. اِشتريتُ حذاءً للرياضةِ وجواربَ جديدة. اِشترتْ
آنّا حذاءً جديداً لأنّها كانتْ بحاجةٍ إليه. قالتْ آنّا إن المدرسةَ مُمْتِعَةٌ.

Sofia　　Mum took me and Anna shopping. She said we had to get special clothes
for school. I got plimsolls for PE and new socks. Anna got new shoes
'cause she needed them. Anna said school is cool.

The night before

صوفيا   قالتْ آنّا إنَّ معلّمتي الآنسةَ روس رائعة. حضَّرْتُ ثيابي لأكونَ جاهزةً بسرعةٍ في الصّباحِ. قالتْ والدتي يجبُ أنْ لا نتأخَّرَ.

Sofia   Anna said that my teacher Miss Ross is *love-e-ly*.
I put out all my clothes so I can get ready quickly in the morning.
Mum said we mustn't be late.

توم

لا يريدُ تيد "الدبدوب" أَنْ يذهبَ إلى المدرسة. قُلتُ لوالدتي إِنَّ تيد يَخافُ أَنْ يَضيعَ.

قالتْ والدتي إِنَّ تيد سيكونُ على ما يرامُ، وأضافتْ أَنَّ تيد سيعرفُ أشخاصاً كثيرينَ مِثلي ومثل صوفيا وآنا. قلتُ لتيد أنّي سأهتَمُّ بِهِ.

Tom   Ted doesn't want to go to school. I told Mum that Ted thinks he'll get lost.
       Mum said Ted will be OK. She said Ted will know lots of people like Sofia
       and Anna and me. I told Ted I'll look after him.

The BIG day

توم سيأخُذُنَا والدي أنا وتيد إلى المدرسةِ. قالَ لي والدي
إنَّهُ يتذكَّرُ أَوَّلَ يومٍ ذهبَ فيهِ إلى المدرسةِ. كيفَ
يُمكِنُهُ تَذَكُّرَ شيئاً حصلَ مُنذُ سِنينَ طويلةٍ؟

Tom   Dad is taking me and Ted to school. Dad said he can remember his first school day. How can he remember something that happened years and years and years ago?

صوفيا إنَّني جاهزةٌ للذّهابِ لكنَّ آنّا غيرُ جاهزةٍ. إنّها لا تزالُ تربطُ ربّاطَ حِذاءِهَا وأنا أُريدُ أَنْ أَذهبَ الآنَ. لا أُريدُ أَنْ أَتأَخَّرَ. طلبت والدتي مِن آنّا أَنْ تُسْرِعَ فقُلتُ أَسرِعي يا آنّا، أُريدُ أَنْ أَذهبَ الآنَ فوراً.

Sofia I'm ready to go and Anna is not. She is doing her laces but I want to go now. I don't want to be late. Mum said hurry up Anna. Hurry up Anna, I want to go NOW!

On the way to school

صوفيا   فتحتْ والدتي البابَ فنزِلْنَا أنا وآنّا السلم بسرعةٍ. وفي الأسفل رأَيْنَا توم وأَباهِ.

Sofia   Mum opened the door and Anna and me raced down the stairs.
             At the bottom we saw Tom and his Dad.

في الطريقِ الى المدرسة

توم   مَشَيْنا أنا وصوفيا وآنّا وأُمُّهُمَا ووالدي وتيد إلى المدرسةِ.
كنتُ أُمْسِكُ بيدِ والدي.
`قالتْ آنّا إنَّ المدرسةَ مُمْتِعَة.

Tom   Sofia and Anna, and their mum and me, and Dad and Ted
walked all the way to school. I held Dad's hand.
Anna said school is cool.

The school

توم

عِندما وَصلْنَا إلى المدرسةِ كانتْ هناكَ سيّدةٌ تنتظِرُنا.
سألتْ عن اِسْمي. أجبْتُ أنَّ اسْمي توم. قالتْ إنَّ اسْمَها
السّيّدَةُ بلام.
اختبأ تيد في جَيْبي.

Tom   When we got to school there was a woman waiting.
       She asked my name. I said Tom. She said her
       name was Mrs Plum.
       Ted hid in my pocket.

في المدرسةِ

صوفيا   عندما وصلْنا إلى المدرسةِ كانَتِ المديرةُ تنتظرُنا.
جاءت لتقول أهلاً للأطفالِ الجُدُدِ. قالتْ آنّا إنَّها تستقبلُنا
هكذا لِتُشْعِرنَا بالتَّرْحَابِ.

Sofia   When we got to school the head teacher was waiting.
She came to say hello to all the new children.
Anna said she does it to make us feel welcome.

Our class

صوفيا   أخذَتْني والدتي إلى صفّنا. كانتِ الآنسةُ روس هناكَ وكانَ
هناكَ أيضاً رجُلٌ يُدْعَى جيم. حَصَلْتُ على علاقةٍ خاصّةً
بِيَّ لأُعَلِّقَ عليها مِعْطَفي وكيسَ الرِّياضةِ. ودَّعَتني والدتي
ولوَّحتْ لي وهي تَخْرُجُ مِنَ البابِ.

Sofia   Mum took me to our class. Miss Ross was there. And a grown-up
called Jim. I got my own peg. That's for my coat and PE bag.
Mum said bye. She waved as she went out of the door.

صَفُّنَا

توم   أخذني والدي إلى صفِّنا فَأَرَيْتُهُ الصّورَةَ التي رَسَمْتُهَا وقلتُ لَهُ إنَّ تيد قلقٍ.
قَالَ والدي إنَّ تيد سيكونُ على ما يرامُ لأنّني بجانِبِهِ وهوَ بجانبي، ثُمَّ
عانَقَني وقالَ لي أنهُ سَيَراني فيما بعدُ. فقلتُ لهُ مَعَ السّلامَةِ.

Tom   Dad took me to our class. I showed Dad my picture. I told Dad Ted was worried.
Dad said Ted would be OK because Ted had me. And I had Ted. Dad gave me a
hug. He said see you later. I said bye.

First lesson

توم

قرَأَتِ الآنسةُ روس لائِحَةَ الحضور. قالتْ
إنّها ستقرَأُ اللائِحَةَ كُلَّ يومٍ وأنَهُ يجبُ علينَا
أنْ نقولَ نعمْ عندمَا تَقرأُ اسْماءَنا.

Tom

Miss Ross called the register. She said
every day she will call the register.
She said we have to say yes when
she calls our name.

صوفيا

قالتِ الآنسةُ روس أن لديْنا الكثيرُ منَ الأعمالِ وأنّ تَأْدِيَةَ هذهِ الأعمالِ مُمْتِعٌ. كانَ أوّلُ عملٍ نقومُ بِهِ هو لُعْبَةَ الأسْماءِ. إنّي أعرفُ أسماءً كثيرةً. صديقَتي اسْمُها زارا.

Sofia   Miss Ross said we had lots of jobs to do. She said doing jobs is fun. Our first job was to play the name game. I know lots of names. Zara is my friend.

Morning break

صوفيا

قالتِ الآنسةُ روس أنّ وقتَ الاسْتِراحةِ قد حان.
ويجب ألا نخرُج فيها لِنَلعَبَ، بَلْ نشربُ الماءَ ونَأْكُلُ الفاكهَةَ.
فجلَسْتُ بجانب زارا وليلي.

Sofia   Miss Ross said now it's break time. We don't go
out to play. We get a drink of water and fruit.
I sat next to Zara and Lili.

استراحَةُ الصّباحِ

توم أثناء الاسْتِراحَةِ يمكِننا الذّهابُ إلى المِرحاضِ فقالتِ الآنسةُ
روس: إِغْسِلوا أَيْدِيكُمْ! ثم قالت: تَذَكَّروا إِقْفَالَ الحَنَفِيَّاتِ.

Tom   At break time we can go to the toilet. Miss Ross said WASH YOUR HANDS.
       Miss Ross said remember to TURN OFF THE TAPS.

توم   َجلَسَ شون بِالقُرْبِ مِنِّي. أَتَمَنّى أَنْ أُعْجِبَهُ.
       رَحَّبَ شون بِيَّ. ثُمَّ قالَ إِنَّ رَسْمَي يُعْجِبَهُ.

Tom   Sean sat next to me. I hope he likes me.
       "Hello!" said Sean. He said he liked my picture.

دُروسٌ أُخْرَى

صوفيا   أَخَذَتِ الآنسةُ روس رَسومَنا وعلَّقَتْهَا على الحائطِ. ثُمَّ لَوَّنْتُ بِطاقَةً كانَ مَكْتُوباً عليها اسمي كَيْ أَلْصقُهَا على جَارُوري.

Sofia

Miss Ross took our pictures and put them on the wall. Then I coloured a card with my name on to put on my drawer.

Lunch time

صوفيا   رَنَّ الْجَرَسُ. أحدث ضجيجاً قَوِيًّا! يَجِبُ عَلَيْنَا أَنْ نَغْسِلَ أَيْدِينَا وَنَصْطَفَّ. أمسَكَتْ زارا بِيَدي. إِنَّها تَأْكُلُ الْوَجْبَةَ الْمَدْرَسِيَّةَ مِثْلِي.

Sofia   A bell rang. It made a BIG noise! We had to wash our hands and line up. Zara held my hand. She has school dinners like me.

توم   أحضر شون غَدَاءً مُعَداً في البيتِ مِثلِي. أخّذناحقائب الغداء وَذَهَبْنَا إلى الصَّالَةِ **الكَبيرَةِ**. كَانَ الضَّجيجُ فيها عالياً. جَلَسْنَا إلى طاولاتٍ طَويلَةٍ. أَكَلْتُ الجُبْنَ والخُبْزَ وتُفَّاحَةً، وَشَرِبْتُ العَصيرَ.

Tom   Sean has packed lunch like me. We got our lunch boxes. We went to the BIG hall. It was very NOISY. We sat at long tables. I had cheese and bread and an apple and juice.

Playtime

توم لعبنَا أنا وشون وليو وأدي لُعْبةَ امسك. كُنَّا نَعْتَبِرُ
المسطبة بَيْتَنَا نَلْجَأ إِلَيْهِ. اِخْتَبَأ تيد في جَيْبِي.

Tom   Sean and Leo and Adi and me played tag. The bench was home.
        Ted hid in my pocket.

وقتُ اللَّعِبِ

صوفيا   لعبْنَا أنا وزارا وليلي القَفْزَ فَوْقَ الْحَبْلِ. وَقَعَتْ ليلي وَجَرَحَتْ رُكْبَتَهَا. احْتَاجَتْ إِلَى ضَمَّادَةٍ. قَالَتْ ليلي أنهَا لَيْسَتْ مُؤلِمة. حقًّا ليلي شُجَاعَةً جِدًّا.

Sofia   Zara and Lili and me played skipping. Lili fell over and hurt her knee.
It needed a plaster. Lili said it doesn't hurt. Lili is very brave.

Story time

صوفيا   جَلَسْنَا جَميعاً على السَّجَّادَةِ وقرأت الآنسةُ روس لَنَا قِصَّةً مِنْ كِتَابٍ كَبيرٍ.

Sofia   We all sat on the carpet. Miss read us a story from a BIG book.

وَقْتُ القِصَّةِ

توم   في نِهايَةِ القِصَّةِ لَعِبْنَا لُعْبَةَ التَّصْفِيقِ وَتَعَلَّمْنَا نشيدَ العَوْدَةِ إِلى البَيْتِ.

Tom   At the end of the story we played a clapping game. We learnt a going home rhyme.

Packing up

توم الَتِ الآنسةُ روس حان وَقْتُ العَوْدَةِ إلى البَيْتِ. وَضَعنا كُلَّ أَشْيائِنَا في جَوارِيرِنَا. أدي له الجَارورُ العُلوي. بَعْدَ ذلِكَ كانَ عَلَيْنَا أَنْ نَصْطَفَّ.

Tom   Miss Ross said hometime. We put all our things in our drawers.
       Adi has the top drawer. Then we had to line up.

صوفيا قَالَتِ الآنسةُ روس حَانَ مَوْعِدُ جَلْبِ مَعَاطِفِنا. رَكَضْنَا نَحْوَ عَلَّاقَاتِنَا.
قَالَتِ الآنسةُ روس **مَمْنُوعٌ الرَكْضُ في المَمَرِّ!** بَدا عَلَيْهَا الاسْتِيَاءُ،
فَعُدْنَا إلى الصَفِّ مَشْياً.

Sofia   Miss Ross said time to get your coats. We ran to our pegs. Miss Ross said
NO RUNNING in the corridor! She looked cross. We walked back to class.

Home time

صوفيا

جاءَتْ آنّا ووالدتي إلى صَفِّي. أَرَيْتُهُمَا الصُّورَةَ التي رَسَمْتُهَا.
قَالَتِ الآنسةُ روس و جيم مَعَ السَّلامَةِ.
فَوَدَّعْتُ زارا وليلي.

Sofia   Mum and Anna came to my class. I showed them
my picture I painted. Miss Ross and Jim said bye.
I said bye to Zara and Lili.

وَقْتُ العَوْدَةِ إِلى البيتِ

توم عِنْدَمَا حَانَ وَقْتُ العَوْدَةِ إِلى البَيْتِ حَضَرَ والِدَيَّ إِلى الصَّفِّ. كَانَتْ لَدَيَّ الكَثِيرَ لأحكيه عَنْ شون وليو وأدي وعَنْ كُلِّ الأَعْمَالِ التي كَانَ عَلَيَّ إِتْمَامُهَا. قَالَ والدِيْ أَنَّني أَصْبَحْتُ تِلْمِيذاً كَبِيراً الآنَ.

Tom   At home time Mum and Dad came to the classroom. I had sooo much to tell about Sean and Leo and Adi and all the jobs I had to do. Dad said I was a big schoolboy now!

توم

تَعَرَّفْتُ على الكَثيرِ مِنَ الأَصْدِقَاءِ. شون صَديقي. وأدي وليو
كَذَلِكَ. شون هو صَديقي المُفَضَّلُ في المَدْرَسَةِ. تيد هو صَديقي
المُفَضَّلُ في البَيْتِ. تيد يُحِبُّ المَدْرَسَةَ وَيُرِيدُ الذَّهَابَ إِلَيْهَا ثَانِيَةً.

Tom   I made lots of friends. Sean is my friend. And Adi and Leo. Sean is my best
       school friend. Ted is my best home friend. Ted likes school. He wants to go again.

البَيْتُ

صوفيا   أكلنا أنا ووالدتي وآنّا الكَعْكَ. لَدَى آنّا واجبات بَيتيَّة. أنا ليس لديَّ واجبات بَيتيَّة. قَالَتْ والدتي من المُمْكِنٌ أَنْ تَزورنا زارا يَوْمَ الجُمْعَةِ بَعدَ المدرسةِ. كَانَتْ آنّا عَلى حَقٍّ – المَدْرَسَةُ مُمْتِعَةٌ.

Sofia   Anna and Mum and me had cake. Anna had homework. I don't have homework. Mum said Zara can come after school on Friday. Anna was right – school is cool.

If you have found this book helpful, there are three more titles in the series that you may wish to try:

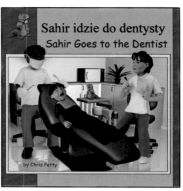

Nita Goes to Hospital
Sahir Goes to the Dentist
Abi Goes to the Doctor

You might like to make your own car, furnish your own house or try out some clothes in the "My...series" CD R

My House
My Car
My Clothes

You may wish to welcome parents and carers in 18 languages with the Welcome Booklet CD Rom Series
where you can publish key information about your school - photos, policies, procedures and people:

Welcome Booklet to My School
Welcome Booklet to My Nursery
All About Me!

First published in 2006 by Mantra Lingua Ltd
Global House, 303 Ballards Lane
London N12 8NP
www.mantralingua.com

A CIP record for this book is available from the British Library